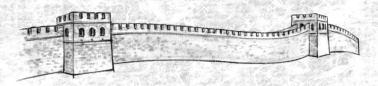

Ancient
CHINESE ART

Jane Shuter

Heinemann
LIBRARY

www.heinemann.co.uk/library
Visit our website to find out more information about Heinemann Library books.

To order:
☎ Phone 44 (0) 1865 888066
🗎 Send a fax to 44 (0) 1865 314091
💻 Visit the Heinemann Bookshop at www.heinemann.co.uk/library to browse our catalogue and order online.

First published in Great Britain by Heinemann Library, Halley Court, Jordan Hill, Oxford, OX2 8EJ, a division of Reed Educational and Professional Publishing Ltd.
Heinemann is a registered trademark of Reed Educational and Professional Publishing Ltd.

OXFORD MELBOURNE AUCKLAND
JOHANNESBURG BLANTYRE GABORONE
IBADAN PORTSMOUTH NH (USA) CHICAGO

Originated by Dot Gradations
Printed in Wing King Tong in Hong Kong

ISBN 0 431 05588 2
05 04 03 02 01
10 9 8 7 6 5 4 3 2 1

British Library Cataloguing in Publication Data

Shuter, Jane
  Ancient Chinese art. - (Art in history)
  1.Art, Ancient - China 2.Art, Chinese - History
  I.Title
  709'.5'1'0901

Acknowledgments

The author and publisher are grateful to the following for permission to use copyright photographs: © Art Archive/British Library, p. 12; © Art Archive/National Palace Museum Taiwan/Harper Collins Publishers, p. 19; © Art Resource, p. 7; © Art Resource/Werner Forman Archive, p. 9; © Art Resource/Werner Forman Archive, p. 27; © Art Resource/Werner Forman Archive, Idemitsu Museum of Art, Tokyo, p. 8; © Art Resource/Werner Forman Archive, National Palace Museum, Taipei, p. 13; © The Bridgeman Art Library Int'l. Ltd. (U.S.)/Private Collection, p. 18; © Corbis/Burstein Collection, pp. 11, 25; © Corbis/Ric Ergenbright, p. 28; © Corbis/Kimbell Art Museum, p. 10; © Corbis/Lowell Georgia, p. 20; © Courtesy of Cultural Relics Publishing House, pp. 4, 5, 22, 23; © The Granger Collection, p. 6; © Idemitsu Museum of Arts, p. 24; © National Geographic Image Collection/O. Louis Mazzatenta, pp. 16, 17; © Nelson-Atkins Museum/The Nelson-Atkins Museum of Art, Kansas City, Missouri (Purchase; Nelson Trust) Photography by Robert Newcombe, p. 29; © NHK (Japan Broadcasting Corporation) & NHK Publishing, p. 26; © Science Museum of London, Science & Society/Picture Collection, p. 14.

Cover photograph reproduced with permission of © Corbis/Lowell Georgia.

Every effort has been made to contact copyright holders of any material reproduced in this book. Any omissions will be rectified in subsequent printings if notice is given to the publisher.

Some words are shown in bold, **like this.** You can find out what they mean by looking in the glossary.

CONTENTS

In this book, dates are followed by the letters BCE (Before Common Era) or CE (Common Era). This is instead of using BC (Before Christ) and AD (*Anno Domini*, meaning in the year of our Lord).

WHAT IS ANCIENT CHINESE ART?

Ancient Chinese art was created between 1500BCE, when China began to be ruled by royal families called **dynasties**, and 1279CE, when the **Mongols** conquered China. This covers almost 3000 years of art, in a country larger than the size of Europe today. It takes several hours to move from one side of Europe to the other by aeroplane, but in ancient Chinese times people walked or rode animals and went much more slowly. Few people travelled over large distances, so Chinese art developed differently in different parts of the country.

Most of the ancient Chinese art that we have comes from the more recent periods. Almost all of the early examples of ancient Chinese art we have are **bronze** pieces, because they survive best. This does not mean that bronze work was the only art produced at this time.

Bronze figure, Sanxingdui, Central China, about 1200BCE, almost 1.8 m high without the base, with the base it is over 2.7 m.

This is the first early bronze to be found that shows a human figure. It was found with several heads made in a similar style. These heads do not look very 'Chinese' and this style did not survive for long. We do not know the names of any of the artists of this period.

How artists worked

Almost all ancient Chinese art before 1000CE was made for a particular person, called a **patron**, who ordered a specific piece. Artists did not create beautiful things and then try to sell them, because materials were too expensive. This did not only apply to painters. Weavers, bronze workers and carvers all worked in the same way.

Emperors set up workshops for weavers, bronze makers and carvers, and regularly ordered paintings from the most highly regarded artists. From the Tang dynasty (618–907CE) onwards, a style of **court art** developed. Painting on **silk scrolls** became popular. Painting and **calligraphy** became fashionable pastimes for important people. Many of the nobles at court, and even the emperors themselves, were artists.

Beaker, ivory inlaid with turquoise, about 1200BCE, 30 cm high.

*Elephants lived in China at the time this beaker was made, so ivory was a local material. The turquoise was a trade item from far away. The beaker was made for the **tomb** of the Shang dynasty queen Fu Hao, who was buried in 1200BCE. It is one of the few surviving pieces of early Chinese art that is not made from bronze. It shows that there were early artists with other skills.*

MATERIALS

Chinese art to us includes many objects the ancient Chinese did not see as art, such as pottery bowls. On the other hand, they saw some things as art that we do not. The ancient Chinese thought that making items such as bowls, screens and statues was a craft skill. They did value beautiful things made by craftspeople, and **emperors** set up workshops where crafts could be made for the court. However, to the ancient Chinese, artists were people who produced paintings, poetry and **calligraphy**. These skills were called 'the three perfections'. Writing was a very important art and included both writing the Chinese characters well and writing a poem to match the feeling in a painting.

Landscape, Ts'ao Chih-po, ink on **silk***, about 1260CE.*

The carefully placed red seals in this painting give the names of various owners of the painting. The seals were not seen as spoiling the picture, but adding to its worth: it showed how many important people had liked it enough to buy it.

Artists' palette

Chinese artists painted with water-based paints and ink. Various natural substances and **pigments** were mixed with water to make paint colours. Powdered clam shells made white; red ochre, a kind of earth, made brown, and some artists even used real silver and gold. Ink was made by mixing soot, the black smut from burning wood, coal, oil or even hair and bones, with glue to make a hard cake. To make ink the artists had to grind off a little of the ink cake, very finely, and mix it with water. Many artists painted only in ink. They thought that the type of soot used and the amount of water added made such differences to the tone of black that there was no need for any other colour. Artists used brushes made from animal hair that came to a very fine point at the tip. This meant they could make very thin lines.

Making your mark

Many early works of art had inscriptions saying who the people in the pictures were. Later, the artists also signed them. Because most art was made to order, the owner of a painting was important. Many pieces of Chinese art are stamped with the seals of their owners. With some pieces of art you can discover how they passed from owner to owner, from when they were first painted to the present day.

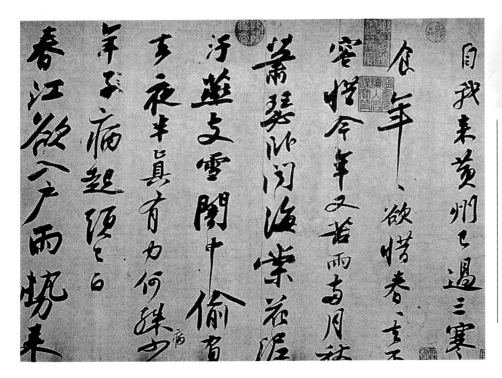

Poem, ink on paper, Song dynasty, about 960–1279CE. The artist and poet who wrote this poem in calligraphy used different parts of his brush to make thick, heavy lines or very thin lines in the characters.

ART AND RELIGION

There were three major religions in ancient China: **Taoism**, **Confucianism** and **Buddhism**. Most of the time they were all accepted, and they all had an important place in ancient Chinese art. A lot of art was made for religious reasons – to be buried in **tombs** or to decorate tombs and temples.

Before 400BCE, **emperors** and other important people had real people buried with them in their tombs to serve them after death. This was because ancient Chinese beliefs about life after death included taking servants and possessions with you into the next world. After 400BCE, the human sacrifices were replaced by terracotta, **earthenware** or **stoneware** figures of servants, animals, houses and entertainers. Tombs and temples were both decorated with wall paintings or carvings. Temples were also decorated on the inside and outside with large statues of important religious figures.

*Musician, terracotta, Han **dynasty** 206BCE–220CE.*

This statue is a model of a musician, made to be put into the tomb of an important person. It shows us how musicians looked and performed in ancient China.

Reproductions of famous art

In 843CE, there was a brief time when Buddhists were **persecuted** in ancient China. Temples, with their beautiful statues and wall paintings, were destroyed. A Tang dynasty writer, called Zhang Yanyuan, was shocked by the loss of the works of art. He decided to make the first art reproduction books, called *Records of Famous Paintings of All the Dynasties*. They had careful reproductions of famous works of art in them, as well as stories about the lives of the artists who painted them and a discussion of various styles of painting. These books contain the only surviving examples of the work of many ancient Chinese artists.

Buddha, rock carving, Yungang caves, Wei Dynasty, about 460–494CE.

The Yungang caves have some of the earliest examples of Buddhist art that exist in China. They were not destroyed in 843CE because the caves are hidden in high cliffs.

PAINTING: LANDSCAPE AND STILL LIFE

The ancient Chinese painted on various surfaces. At first, they painted on walls, wood or, less often, on **silk**. From 300BCE silk **scrolls** became the most common surface to paint on. It was not until after 1000CE that paper was widely used. Both paper and silk were first treated with an **alum** wash, to stop the ink from **bleeding** too much. Chinese artists, unlike Western ones, painted the **foreground** first and then worked back, doing the **background** last. Once they were dry, paintings were given another coat of alum to set the colours.

The Song **dynasty** painter, Guo Xi, said 'landscape paintings must show a harmonious relationship between earth and heaven'. The ancient Chinese wanted their paintings to show nature, but nature controlled and in order, not nature as it appeared around them. Early landscape painters included people or buildings, though they were shown very small. The most harmonious landscape would show both earth and water, because this produced a balance of the earth and water elements.

Landscape in the style of Tung Yuan, by Wen Chia, ink on paper, about 1577CE, 167 cm by 52 cm.

The artist of this landscape copied the techniques used in the Song dynasty. It follows the rules written by Xie He.

The six rules of painting

The ancient Chinese developed rules for painting. Of course, no one had to follow them, but the most admired paintings were the ones that followed these rules. The rules were outlined by Xie He in about 500CE:

1 The painting must have vitality (liveliness).
2 The brush must be used properly.
3 The painting must show accurately what is painted.
4 The right colours must be used in the right order.
5 Things must be arranged harmoniously in the painting.
6 A painter should learn by copying. When you copy a painting make sure it is accurate, in the spirit of the first painting and respectful of the first painter.

Many things used in landscape and still-life painting were **symbolic**. Snow symbolized purity, bamboo showed strength and plum blossom meant simplicity. Dragons were not supposed to be frightening, as they are in many Western cultures. To the ancient Chinese they symbolized strength, wisdom, luck and goodness.

Painting of Bamboo, painting on silk, Yuan Dynasty, about 1260–1368CE.

*The **patron** who commissioned this painting wanted people who saw it to think he was a strong person. The ancient Chinese audience would understand that the bamboo in the picture was a symbol of strength, as well as being a beautiful image.*

PAINTING: PEOPLE AND ANIMALS

Ancient Chinese artists preferred to portray calm, still scenes. Frantic movement and violent emotions were seen as things that quickly passed and that were not admirable. Even when they painted busy town scenes or crowds of people in motion, there is still a feeling of calm in ancient Chinese pictures, and a sense that every person in them is going about his or her business in an organized and purposeful way. There is a sense of order and control, just as there is in the landscape paintings.

*Portrait of Empress Wu Zeitan, the wife of **Emperor** Gaozong Tang, painting on silk, 18th-century copy of a painting from about 705CE.*

Wu Zeitan was the first Empress of China. She lived from 624CE to 705CE. This picture was probably used for **ancestor** worship, an important ceremony for the ancient Chinese.

Accurate images
Unlike the ancient Egyptians, the ancient Chinese did not try to show a perfect version of a person or animal in a painting. They wanted to make an accurate picture that would capture the spirit of the person or animal. The artist who painted Empress Wu Zeitan included her wrinkles to make the picture accurate.

Gu Kaizhi

Zhang Yanyuan called Gu Kaizhi 'the father of Chinese painting' in his illustrated book of Chinese art in 847CE. Gu lived from about 345CE to 406CE. During his life, he had been considered an important artist by some people, but his fame increased after his death. By the time of the Tang **dynasty,** when Zhang was writing, Gu was widely respected and his paintings were frequently copied. Gu was important because, while he used traditional subjects and poses for his paintings, he used a more realistic style than earlier artists. His animals and people seem alive and are often painted as though the artist caught them just as they were about to do something. By the Tang period Gu was being given almost sole credit for the move towards accurately representing subjects in a painting.

Two Horses and a Groom, *copy of a painting by Gu Kaizhi, painting on silk, about 700–800CE.*

It looks as if the **groom** *has just pulled the reign on the horse he is riding, causing it to turn and look at the viewer, while the horse in the foreground turns to see why the other horse moved. These kinds of realistic reactions are examples of Gu's innovative realistic style.*

BRONZES

Bronze working is almost the only form of art to survive from earliest times to the present day. The first bronze workers made large, heavy, beautifully decorated bronze pieces for use in burials. At first, the various royal **dynasties** seem to have controlled bronze making. It is possible that the imposing bronze pieces were seen as something that only important people should own. Later bronze workers made much more delicate objects. Some of these smaller objects were simply decorative, but some were useful, too.

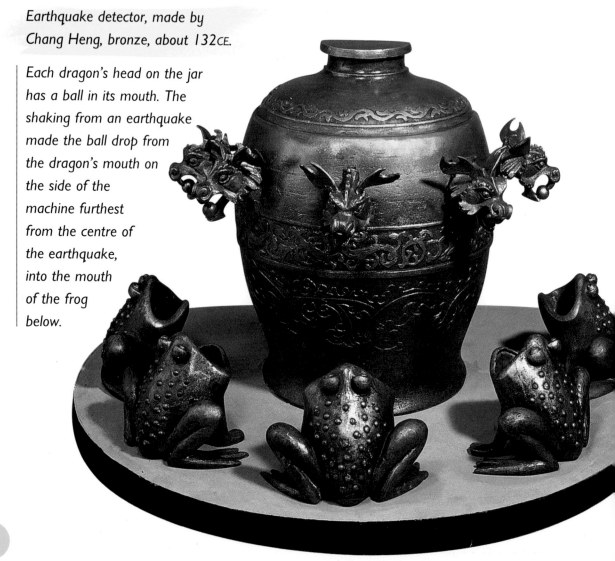

Earthquake detector, made by Chang Heng, bronze, about 132CE.

Each dragon's head on the jar has a ball in its mouth. The shaking from an earthquake made the ball drop from the dragon's mouth on the side of the machine furthest from the centre of the earthquake, into the mouth of the frog below.

The lost wax method

The lost wax method of making bronze enabled ancient Chinese artists to produce whole objects covered with lots of detail. These are the stages:

1 The artist made a wax model of his work. This could be very simple, with smooth flowing lines, or very detailed.
2 The artist covered the wax model in a thick layer of wet clay, leaving a large hole at the top and several small holes at the bottom. The clay was left to dry.
3 When the artist was sure that the clay was dry, he heated up the clay. As the heat worked through to the centre, the wax melted and trickled out of the holes at the bottom of the clay mould.
4 Once all the wax was out of the mould, the artist plugged the hole in the bottom of the clay mould. He then poured in melted bronze. Because the bronze was runny, it filled in all the spaces left by the wax.
5 The artist left the mould while the bronze set, then broke it open and took out the finished bronze.

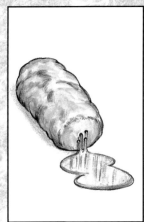
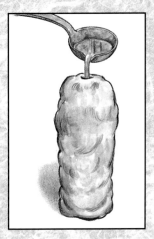

Using bronze as glue

Early bronzes were made in pieces, which were then carefully joined together using freshly heated bronze as glue. Each piece was made by pouring melted bronze between two clay pieces. One piece was smooth, to produce the smooth inside of the bronze piece. The pattern of the bronze was made on the other side, but reversed so that where the clay pattern stood out the bronze pattern went in. From 500BCE onwards, bronze workers began to use the lost wax method for making bronze pieces which meant they could make pieces that were even more beautiful and complicated.

TERRACOTTA

Terracotta is made from clay mixed with water, which is then moulded and baked at around 900° C – three times hotter than the hottest setting on your kitchen oven! Terracotta was used mainly for simple things such as everyday pottery or roof tiles. It was also used to make models of houses, animals and people to bury in **tombs**. However, some important people were buried with life-size models.

In 1974, **archaeologists** working near the mound where the **emperor** Sui Huangdi of the Qin **dynasty** (221–206BCE) is buried, found a pit containing the first soldiers of a life-size terracotta army. The pits are still being excavated, but archaeologists think there are 7000 soldiers in total. The people who made them would have included artists to produce moulds, workmen to make the pieces, builders to make and repair the

kilns used to bake the warriors, metalworkers to make the weapons, and a huge army of workers to collect and deliver the firewood needed to keep the kilns hot.

Archer, terracotta, Terracotta Army of Sui Huangdi, about 210BCE.

This life-size archer's hands are empty, but when he was made he would have been holding real arrows and a real bow. All the terracotta warriors were armed with real weapons. Tomb robbers stole many of these soon after the emperor was buried. Some of the weapons left behind must have been specially treated to prevent rusting, as they are still shiny and sharp after more than 2000 years.

Mass production

The terracotta army is one of the earliest examples of **mass-produced** art, as it is made from a limited number of parts, joined together in various combinations. For example, for the standing warriors, which were about 1.8 m tall, there were three styles of plinth (base) for the warriors to stand on, two different styles of legs, eight different body shapes, two different sorts of arms, several styles of hand (with the fingers made separately and added in different combinations) and eight different heads. The facial features and hairstyles were finished by hand to make the soldiers look less mass-produced.

In this picture it is possible to see both how the warriors were mass-produced, and the ways they were individualized.

17

POTTERY

Chinese potters made beautiful bowls, jars, plates and other objects. There were two main types: **earthenware**, which was **fired** at 800° C, and pottery that was baked at a much higher temperature. (Westerners divided Chinese pottery into three types: earthenware, **stoneware**, and **porcelain**.) Earthenware is pottery fired at a high temperature that is any colour from black to grey inside, and porcelain is pottery fired at such a high temperature that it is pure white inside. Westerners valued porcelain highly because they did not know what was added to the clay to made it white when it was fired. This made porcelain very valuable to the Chinese as a trade item.

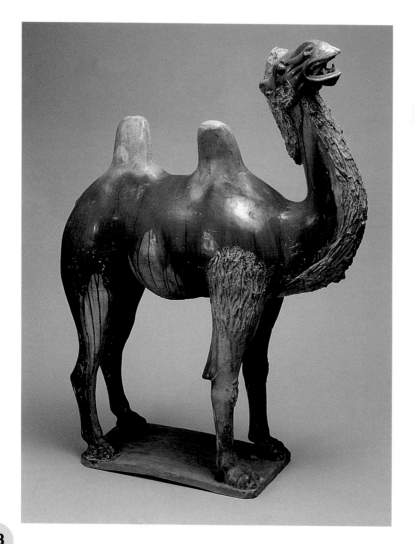

*Camel **tomb** model, earthenware, about 618–906CE.*

The ancient Chinese used camels for carrying goods on long trips. During the Tang dynasty, tomb models became more carefully detailed and glazed. They were used in more tombs too, not just the tombs of important people. Most pottery sculptures were made of earthenware, stoneware or terracotta because they were less expensive than porcelain.

What made porcelain special?

Porcelain was especially hard and smooth, as well as white. It could be made much thinner than other pottery, too. Good porcelain was very thin. In 851CE a visitor to China from the Middle East, called Suliman, remarked, 'The Chinese have a fine clay which they make into vessels equal in quality to glass, for you can see the liquid they hold inside them.'

The ingredients that gave porcelain its special qualities were a white clay, called kaolin, mixed with a rock called petuntse. Petuntse was also added to the glaze used to coat porcelain. It made the glaze harden quickly, and made it harder to chip. Porcelain was traded widely, and was very valuable both in China and in the West.

*Ju porcelain, Song **dynasty**, about 1086CE–1106CE.*

*Porcelain made in the kilns at Ju is rare now. It was made for just 20 years, between 1086CE and 1106CE. All the porcelain made there was made for the **imperial** court.*

The secret of porcelain

Europeans discovered the secret of porcelain by accident. Johann Bottger, a young man who said he thought he knew how to turn metal into gold, had been put in prison by Augustus II, King of Poland. Augustus wanted the secret as soon as Bottger found it. Instead, while firing earth at high temperatures, Bottger discovered porcelain. He was put in charge of the first European porcelain factory in Meissen, Germany.

RELIEF CARVING

The ancient Chinese made carved stone slabs, intended mainly to go on **tomb** walls or on the walls of **shrines** to important people. Carvers began to work in stone when these tombs started to have public areas where visitors could come, probably to pay their respects to the dead person buried or remembered there. These carvings are called **reliefs**. They are carved so that the design is raised from the background. The carvers always used similar scenes, and modern Chinese historians think that these are intended to link ideas about the afterlife to ideas about social order on earth. A battle scene would show both a battle on earth, **symbolic** of social disorder, as well as chaos and order battling for the dead man's soul in the afterlife.

Rubbing of a stone slab relief, from the Shrine of Wu Ban, Jiaxing, northeast China, about 147CE.

A series of shrines devoted to the important Wu family were built at Jiaxing. No one was ever buried at the shrines, but the carvers used the same ideas and images as they did for tomb carvings. They also carved images of everyday life, like this one, from which we can find out about how the ancient Chinese were dressed.

Make your own wall relief

Stone carving took a long time and could be very expensive. Brick reliefs were also made to decorate stone walls. The design was drawn up and marked into brick-sized rectangles. Moulds were made to stamp the design onto each brick. The bricks were then fired one by one, and built up to make the original design.

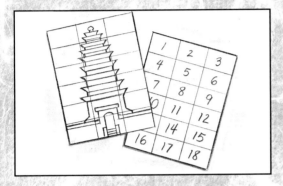

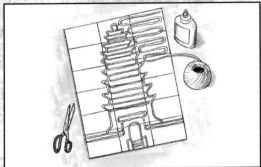

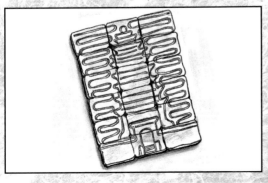

You will need:

cardboard	glue
pencil	ruler
scissors	modelling
string	clay

1 Take a piece of card 30 cm by 30 cm. Draw a design on it. Keep it simple the first time!

2 Mark the design into bricks 7.6 cm by 5 cm.

3 Number the back of each brick, so you know where it goes in the picture.

4 Glue string to the parts of the design that you want to be the background. You may need to mark your brick lines over the string in places. Leave your wall to dry.

5 Cut carefully along the brick-marking lines.

6 Make 24 bricks 7.6 cm by 5 cm out of modelling clay.

7 Use your card bricks to print your design onto the clay bricks. Keep your matching clay brick and your numbered card brick together.

8 Build your clay wall, using the numbers on the card bricks as a guide.

LACQUER AND JADE

Ancient Chinese artists made beautiful objects with lacquer and jade from the earliest times. In both cases, the work was difficult and time consuming.

Jade is an extremely hard stone. There were two types of jade, nephrite and jadeite. Neither could be found in China, so they had to be traded with other countries. Nephrite was the most valued kind of jade. It came in green, brown, beige and white. All jade was so hard that it could not be carved in the way other stones were carved. Jade workers had to use very strong tools to make a rough shape and then do the actual carving by rubbing the shape with a powdered mineral called quartzite. The rubbing process took much longer than ordinary carving. Even a simple bracelet could take several days.

Immortal on horseback, white jade, about 70BCE, 8.9 cm long and 7 cm high.

White jade was the most beautiful of all jade to the ancient Chinese. This carving shows a mythical figure on horseback. It comes from the tomb of the Han emperor, Zhaodi, who died in about 70BCE.

Lacquer working

Lacquer is made from the sap of the lacquer tree, a relative of the poison ivy plant. The sap is drained off and can be coloured with various **pigments** and used like paint or varnish. It can be painted onto various surfaces, including wood, baskets and stone. When dry, it is heat- and water-resistant and very shiny. This makes it practical. It is also very beautiful, especially when colours are built up in many layers to produce pictures that have great depth. Each coat of lacquer takes about two days to dry. Some of the most beautiful pieces of lacquer work, made for **emperors** and very expensive, can have as many as 200 coats of lacquer. Lacquer artists had to be very careful workers. Mistakes on any of the layers could ruin the whole piece.

Screen, wood and lacquer, about 484BCE, 79 cm high.

*This screen is from the tomb of Sima Jinlong. The Sima family was an important family in northern China. The pictures on the screen are copies of **silk scroll** paintings by Gu Kaishi. As everyone sat on cushions or mats on the floor, the screen, which was a room divider, did not need to be very high.*

23

CALLIGRAPHY

Ancient Chinese writing began as picture writing. Each picture stood for a particular object, action or emotion. These pictures are much more recognizable in very early pieces of writing – the character for a house really looks like one. As time passed and people wrote more, they changed the characters and five main **calligraphy** types developed:

1 *Zhuan shu,* the first written language to be used all over China, was developed in 221 BCE by the First **Emperor**. It stayed in use on the seals that the ancient Chinese used as personal signatures.
2 *Li shu* was developed in about 200 BCE, during the Han **dynasty**, for record keeping.
3 *Kai shu* was developed in about 250 BCE for ordinary writing. It is the most common writing today, and is the script used for printed books.
4 *Xing shu* was developed in about 300 BCE as artistic writing. This is the writing that was used on paintings and was considered an art form.
5 *Cao shu* was developed in about 650 BCE for making notes. It is the quickest to write, but the least beautiful.

Mountain Market in a Clearing Mist, *Yujian, ink on paper, about 1250 CE.*

This painting was by the **Buddhist** *monk Yujian. The writing on it is a poem in* xing shu *writing.*

Five-coloured Parakeet on a Branch of Apricot Blossom, *Emperor Hui Tsung, painting on* **silk**, *about 1100CE–1135CE.*

This painting includes a calligraphy poem. The artist has painted the calligraphy characters as carefully and perfectly as the image of the parakeet.

Perfect characters

Ancient Chinese calligraphy was seen as an art form because the aim was to make each character perfect, which was very hard to do. You had to hold your brush in the right way, load it with just the right amount of ink, make the brush strokes in the right direction and keep each brush stroke for each character in proportion with all the others. Each character had to be copied over and over again. The Chinese still try to make perfect characters today. Many art shops sell Chinese brushes, inks and books that show how to paint the various characters. Some libraries have books on Chinese painting, too. It takes a great deal of patience and copying to get even simple brush stokes just right.

TEMPLES

The ancient Chinese believed in spirits and demons that could affect everyday life. They also believed in **ancestor** worship and thought their ancestors' spirits could affect everyday life. **Emperors** and their ancestors were worshipped, too. Religion and everyday behaviour were linked together, and Chinese families had **shrines** in their homes where they could worship. Temples where **monks** and others could meditate and worship were also built. Many temples were created in caves, which were beautifully decorated. There were huge carvings of spirits, demons and teachers. These were linked to both **Buddhism** and **Taoism**.

Paintings in the Mogao Caves, Dunhuang, China, about 538CE. This is the interior of cave number 285.

*The eleven colours used to decorate this cave include expensive mineral **pigments** from far away. The artists who painted them were craftsmen employed by the state, and were not allowed to work for anyone else. Their work was probably passed down from father to son. They worked constantly in the complex of caves, repairing crumbling stone and renewing the paint.*

Shrines

Shrines were often dedicated to ancestors of important families. In some cases, like the Wu shrines in Jianxing, there were several shrines to different members of the same family. Shrines were also built for one especially powerful member of a royal family, who was seen as having a great influence on everyday life. An example of this is a shrine to the Sage Mother, an early Zhou empress. It was beautifully decorated and had a huge painted statue of the Sage Mother and several small statues of ladies in waiting. As well as being worshipped as an ancestor, the Sage Mother was worshipped as a goddess who could bring rain. Shrines did not have artists working full-time. Artists were brought in when there was work to do.

Qiyun 'Cloud Reaching' Pagoda, Luoyang, China, about 1175CE.

Pagodas were a form of Buddhist temple with roofs in many storeys. The number of storeys on a pagoda is based on numbers that were important in the Buddhist religion. Pagodas did not replace cave temples. They were built when a tall and graceful temple was more suitable for the landscape.

BUILDINGS

The ancient Chinese built beautiful houses and gardens, too. The various **emperors** and their families had the most beautiful homes. Their palaces were built inside high walls and were huge, with courtyards, gardens and lakes. From the time of the First Emperor onwards, emperors also had various large building projects, such as roads, canals and, most famous of all, the Great Wall.

The Great Wall of China, about 1350CE, about 2700 km long

The Great Wall was built with various materials, depending on what the builders could find in each local area. Much of the wall was made with packed earth, sometimes with layers of reeds too, to absorb moisture. In the Gobi desert, local plants and sand or stones were used; in other places, logs and clay. In all cases, the materials had to be solidly packed down before the builders added the next layer.

Tower house tomb model, stoneware, about 206BCE–221CE.

This tomb model shows a walled tower house and its courtyard and main gates. Many homes were only one storey and extended away from the main entrance. Tower houses were built in cities with lots of people, where space was a problem. From the model you can see that artists carved and painted the outside walls of the houses, as well as the inside walls and the gates.

Homes

There are no **imperial** palaces still standing from the ancient Chinese period, although some have been **excavated**. There are no accurate paintings either. Imperial palaces were private, since the royal family did not want people to know how they lived. This created a custom of keeping homes private that was soon followed by all people, from emperors to city tradesmen. Most houses had a central space open to the sky, which they called the 'well of heaven'. The houses of wealthy families had several courtyards. The further away from the main double gates you went, the more private the parts of the house were. Homes were built using wood, and roofs were covered with terracotta tiles. Inside spaces were divided up by screens that were often beautifully carved, lacquered, or painted.

TIMELINE

BCE

1766–1122	The Shang dynasty rules China
about1400	Artists begin bronze working in China
about1300	Writing begins to be used in China
about1200	Queen Fu Hao is buried
	Painting on plaster walls begins
	The Sanxingdui bronzes are made
1122–480	The Zhou dynasty rules China
	Many large bronze objects are found in burials of this time
551–479	Confucius lives and teaches in China
about 300	Silk is first used as a painting and writing surface at this time
480–221	The Warring States period – during this time different parts of China are ruled by different dynasties, and it is not united
221–206	The Qin dynasty rules China
about 220	Writing is standardized across China by the First Emperor
about 201	A terracotta army is made for tomb of the First Emperor
	The first Great Wall of China is built around this time
206	The Han dynasty begins to rule China

CE

220	The Han dynasty ends its rule of China
about 100	Paper is invented by the Chinese
about 100	Buddhism becomes an important religion in China
220–581	Various dynasties – during this time different parts of China are ruled by different dynasties, and the country is not united
about 345 – about 406	Gu Kaizhi lives and works in China
about 500	Xie He writes the Six Laws of Painting
538/539	The earliest dated painted temple cave is completed at Dunhang
	Trade with the West via the Silk Road allows Westerners to appreciate Chinese art
581–618	The Sui dynasty rules China
about 600	Porcelain is invented and perfected in China
618–907	The Tang dynasty rules China
845–847	Buddhism is temporarily persecuted, and much art is destroyed
847	Zhang Yangyun produces books with pictures of the art of the great artists
907–960	Five Dynasties – during this time different parts of China are ruled by different dynasties, and the country is not united
960–1279	The Song Dynasty rules China
984	The emperor sets up an official Imperial Painting Academy
about 1000	Paper is first used as a painting surface

GLOSSARY

alum powder made of chemicals and minerals that can be sprinkled over ink or paint to dry it

ancestor someone who lived before you in your family, such as a grandparent

archaeologist person who studies the past by looking at monuments and objects linked to certain cultures

background part of a painting that seems furthest away, and sets the scene of the painting

bleeding when ink blots on a surface and looks fuzzy

bronze metal that is a mixture of copper and tin

Buddhism religion based on the teachings of Buddha

calligraphy writing made with artistic lettering

Confucianism set of beliefs based on the writings of Confucius

court art art created for the emperor, nobles and other important people in the imperial palace

dynasty kings and queens in the same family

earthenware pottery fired at low temperatures that cannot hold water unless it is glazed

excavated uncovered by an archaeologist

emperor ruler of a dynasty

firing baking clay to make it able to hold water

foreground the part of a painting that looks as if it is at the front of the picture

groom person who is employed to take care of someone's horses

immortal lives forever

imperial having to do with the emperor

mass production making a lot of things that look exactly the same at once

Mongol person from Mongolia, a country that was next to China

monk man who gives up his job and family to devote his life to religion

patron person who orders art, so the artist can be sure of payment when the work is finished

persecute to harass people because of their religious beliefs

pigment coloured material taken from animals, plants, earth, or rocks, and used to make paint or dye

porcelain pottery made from kaolin and petuntse and fired at a high temperature

relief carving with some figures raised to stand out from the surface

scroll roll of material, such as paper or silk, used for writing and painting on

shrine place that is dedicated to a religious figure and used for worship. A shrine is often smaller than a temple.

silk cloth made of the material that silkworms make to build cocoons

symbolic when a picture of something suggests something else.

Taoism religion based on the ideas of Lao-tzu combined with the ideas of Buddha

tomb place where dead people are buried, often elaborately decorated

INDEX